# RAF, Dominion & Allied Squadrons at War:
# Study, History and Statistics

### Compiled by
### Phil H. Listemann
Drawings by Chris Thomas

### Preface

The purpose of this study is to provide aviation historians and enthusiasts with a range of information relative to each of the Commonwealth squadrons that saw combat during World War II. Each record will comprise a short history, complete with illustrations and artwork, and accompanied by the following appendices:

*Appendix I*: Squadron Commanders and Flight Commanders
*Appendix II*: Major awards
*Appendix III*: Operational diary (number of sorties per month)
*Appendix IV*: Victory list
*Appendix V*: Aircraft losses on operations
*Appendix VI*: Aircraft losses in accidents
*Appendix VII*: Aircraft Serial numbers matching with individual letters (including mission totals for multi-engine aircraft)
*Appendix VIII*: Nominal roll (Captains only for bomber and seaplane units)
*Appendix IX*: Roll of Honour

Individual files will be constantly updated, when any fresh information comes to light. Additional information will be available for download, at no charge, on each squadron's site at:

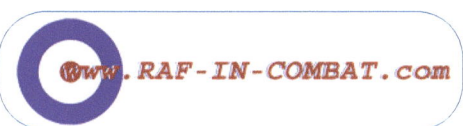

### Glossary of Terms

#### Ranks

AC: Aircraftman
G/C: Group Captain
W/C: Wing Commander
S/L: Squadron Leader
F/L: Flight Lieutenant
F/O: Flying Officer
P/O: Pilot Officer
W/O: Warrant Officer
F/Sgt: Flight Sergeant
Sgt: Sergeant
Cpl: Corporal
LAC: Leading Aircraftman

#### Other

AAF: Auxiliary Air Force
CO: Commanding Officer
DFC: Distinguished Flying Cross
DFM: Distinguished Flying Medal
DSO: Distinguished Service Order
Eva.: Evaded
Inj.: Injured
ORB: Operational Record Book
OTU: Operational Training Unit
PAF: Polish Air Force
PoW: Prisoner of War
RAF: Royal Air Force
RAAF: Royal Australian Air Force
RCAF: Royal Canadian Air Force
RNZAF: Royal New Zealand Air Force
SAAF: South African Air Force
Sqn: Squadron
TOC: Taken on charge
†: Killed

# No. 168 Squadron 1942-1945

# ISBN: 978-2-918590-64-4

*Contributors & Acknowledgments:*

*Andrew Thomas, Chris Thomas, Roger Wallsgrove (Text consultant).*

**Copyright**

**© 2011 Philedition - Phil H. Listemann**

**revised 2015**

All right reserved. No part of this book may be reproduced, stored in a retrieval system or transmitted in any form by any means, electronic, mechanical, photocopying, recording or otherwise, without prior permission of the author.

*Cover: F/L Bolton is ready to take-off from B.-21 in Normandy in board of Mustang AM101/K*

## Main Equipment

| | |
|---|---|
| Tomahawk I | Jun.42 - Mar.43 |
| Tomahawk IIA | Jun.42 - Mar.43 |
| Tomahawk IIB | Nov.42 - Sep.43 |
| Mustang I | Nov.42 - Aug.43 |
| Mustang IA | Jun.43 - Jun.44 |
| Mustang I | Feb.44 - Oct.44 |
| Typhoon IB | Sep.44 - Feb.45 |

## Squadron Code Letters:

**Tomahawk:**

**EK** later **OE**

**Mustang:**

**OE** then nil

**Typhoon:**

**QC**

## Squadron History

Never formed or planned to be formed in World War One, this squadron was formed at Snailwell on **15 June 1942** as tactical reconnaissance unit from a nucleus provided by No.268 Squadron. Its initial equipment was Tomahawks, but they were used for training only and for combined exercises with the Army. The Mustang Mk.I arrived in November and the following month the first operational sortie was carried out by F/L P.W. Mason on 7 December, a *Rhubarb* sortie over the Rouen area, flown with No.613 Squadron.

However, most of the squadron's activities which followed remained exercises with the Army in preparation for the planned invasion of Europe. Until disbandment of the Army-Cooperation Command and the integration into the 2nd Tactical Air Force in July 1943, less than 60 sorties were carried out and two aircraft and pilots lost. Forming part of No.123 Airfield (later No.123 Wing), the squadron began regular reconnaissance operations (code named *Popular*) over the continent, first with Mustang Mk.Is, later with the four-cannon version the Mk.IA, before returning to the Mk.I in Febrruary 1944. Up to D-Day, about 700 sorties were carried out under No.39 (Recce) Wing authority, for the loss of ten Mustangs and six pilots killed.

Following the invasion, the squadron moved to France and provided tactical reconnaissance to No.21 Army Group. Throughout the liberation of France and then Holland the squadron was intensively called upon to perform tactical reconnaissance sorties and up to end of September 1944 over 1,500 sorties were carried out for the loss of 17 Mustangs and five pilots killed while its CO, S/L D.W. Barlow was taken prisoner on 13 August 1944. On 25 September the first two Typhoons arrived and the last Mustang sorties were flown five days later. In October 1944, the squadron moved to Holland fully equipped with Typhoons and was placed under No.143 (RCAF) Wing authority, with the mission to protect the other Typhoons of the Wing, an unusual role for the aircraft, generally used in fighter-bomber missions at this stage of war. It thus became the only Typhoon unit not to carry any rockets or bombs during their missions. The squadron began armed reconnaissance sorties over Germany and provided escorts to daylight bombing raids during the month and in six months and close to 1,000 sorties, the Squadron was able to destroy four enemy aircraft in the air including one during the German air strike of Bodenplatte on 1 January 1945. They sustained heavy losses in return, including the new CO on 3 February 1945, S/L E.C.H. Vernon-Jarvis. The squadron officially disbanded on **26 February 1945** but continued to operate for a further two days before being grounded for the last time. It was the first Typhoon unit to be disbanded and its tally stopped at about 3,200 sorties, 4 aircraft destroyed for the loss of 21 pilots killed, all but two in operations, and three pilots taken prisoners, a high toll for its contribution to the liberation of Europe.

## Squadron Bases

| | | | | | |
|---|---|---|---|---|---|
| Snailwell | 15.06.42 - 13.07.42 | Llandbedr | | | 21.01.44 - 03.02.44 |
| Bottisham | 13.07.42 - 18.11.42 | North Weald | | | 03.02.44 - 06.03.44 |
| Odiham | 18.11.42 - 01.03.43 | Gatwick | | | 06.03.44 - 31.03.44 |
| Weston Zoyland | 01.03.43 - 17.03.43 | Odiham | | | 31.03.44 - 29.06.44 |
| Odiham | 17.03.43 - 20.09.43 | B.8 Sommervieu (France) | | | 29.06.44 - 14.08.44 |
| Hutton Cranswick | 20.03.43 - 10.10.43 | B.21 St.Honorine de Ducy (France) | | | 14.08.44 - 01.09.44 |
| Huggate | 10.10.43 - 15.10.43 | B.34 Avrilly (France) | | | 01.09.44 - 20.09.44 |
| Thruxton | 15.10.43 - 12.11.43 | B.66 Blakenberg (Belgium) | | | 21.09.44 - 04.10.44 |
| Sawbridgworth | 12.11.43 - 30.11.43 | B-78 Eindhoven (Netherlands) | | | 04.10.44 - 26.02.45 |
| North Weald | 30.11.43 - 21.01.44 | | | | |

## APPENDIX I
### SQUADRON AND FLIGHT COMMANDERS

| | | | |
|---|---|---|---|
| S/L George F. **WATSON-SMYTH** | RAF No.25069 | RAF | 15.06.42 - 14.08.42 |
| S/L Richard I.M. **BOWEN** | RAF No.25118 | RAF | 14.08.42 - 28.04.43 |
| S/L Percy W. **MASON** | RAF No.41721 | RAF | 28.04.43 - 07.08.44 |
| S/L Druce W. **BARLOW** (PoW) | RAF No.43527 | RAF | 07.08.44 - 13.08.44 |
| S/L Derek A.D.L. **NICHOLS** (Temp.) | RAF No.72002 | RAF | 14.08.44 - 02.10.44 |
| S/L Leonard H. **LAMBERT** | RAF No.119791 | RAF | 02.10.44 - 02.02.45 |
| S/L Eric C.H. **VERNON-JARVIS** (†) | RAF No.65545 | RAF | 02.02.45 - 03.02.45 |
| S/L Leonard H. **LAMBERT** | RAF No.119791 | RAF | 04.02.45 - 26.02.45 |

#### A FLIGHT

| | | | |
|---|---|---|---|
| F/L Percy W. **MASON** | RAF No.41721 | RAF | 15.06.42 - 07.05.43 |
| F/L Peter D. **MORRIS** | RAF No.43551 | RAF | 07.05.43 - 04.08.43 |
| F/L Michael A. **RICHARDSON** | RAF No.115442 | RAF | 07.08.43 - 22.07.44 |
| F/L Druce W. **BARLOW** | RAF No.43527 | RAF | 22.07.44 - 07.08.44 |
| F/L Charles A.McC. **BARBOUR** | RAF No.120863 | RAF | 07.08.44 - 28.10.44 |
| F/L Peter **EDELSTEN** | RAF No.128855 | RAF | 28.10.44 - 26.02.45 |

#### B FLIGHT

| | | | |
|---|---|---|---|
| F/L Frederick N. **BANTFOFT** | RAF No.44534 | RAF | 15.06.42 - 03.05.43 |
| F/L Michael J. **GRAY** | RAF No.106182 | RAF | 03.05.43 - 07.06.43 |
| F/L Robert R. **SANDERSON** | Aus.400836 | RAAF | 22.06.43 - 28.05.44 |
| F/L Leonard H. **LAMBERT** | RAF No.119791 | RAF | 28.05.44 - 02.10.44 |
| F/L John D. **STUBBS** (†) | Aus.413275 | RAAF | 02.10.44 - 02.01.45 |
| F/L Donald E. **LOVE** | RAF No.128128 | RAF | 03.01.45 - 04.02.45 |
| F/L John B.C. **CATTERNS** | RAF No.144938 | RAF | 05.02.45 - 26.02.45 |

## APPENDIX II
### MAJOR AWARDS

**DSO: -**

**DFC: 11**

Charles Alan McCall **BARBOUR** (No.120863 - RAF)
Desmond Alan **CLIFTON-MOGG** (No.122932 - RAF)
Michael John **GRAY** (No.106182 - RAF)
Leonard Horace **LAMBERT** (No.119791 - RAF)
Roderick Maton **MACKENZIE** (Aus.413242 - RAAF)
Percy Walter **MASON** (No.41721 - RAF)
Harold James **PANITZKI** (Aus.408211 - RAAF)
John Edward **PERKINS** (No.124852 - RAF)
Michael Alan **RICHARDSON** (No.115442 - RAF)
Robert Reginald **SANDERSON** (Aus.400836 - RAAF)
John Douglas **STUBBS** (Aus.413275 - RAAF)

**DFM: -**

## APPENDIX III
### OPERATIONAL DIARY
### NUMBER OF SORTIES PER MONTH

| Date | Month | Total |
|---|---|---|
| Dec.42 | 2 | 2 |
| Jan.43 | 21 | 23 |
| Feb.43 | 5 | 28 |
| Mar.43 | - | 28 |
| Apr.43 | 18 | 46 |
| May.43 | 18 | 64 |
| Jun.43 | 105 | 169 |
| Jul.43 | 29 | 198 |
| Aug.43 | 31 | 229 |
| Sep.43 | 58 | 287 |
| Oct.43 | 2 | 289 |
| Nov.43 | 34 | 323 |
| Dec.43 | 54 | 377 |
| Jan.44 | 35 | 412 |
| Feb.44 | 69 | 481 |
| Mar.44 | 61 | 542 |
| Apr.44 | 79 | 621 |
| May.44 | 142 | 763 |
| Jun.44 | 315 | 1,078 |
| Jul.44 | 492 | 1,570 |
| Aug.44 | 506 | 2,076 |
| Sep.44 | 126 | 2,202 |
| Oct.44 | 169 | 2,371 |
| Nov.44 | 205 | 2,576 |
| Dec.44 | 220 | 2,796 |
| Jan.45 | 163 | 2,959 |
| Feb.45 | 228 | 3,187 |
| **Grand Total** | **3,187** | **3,187** |

Extracted from AIR27/1093

## APPENDIX IV
### VICTORY LIST
### CONFIRMED (C) AND PROBABLE (P) CLAIMS

**TYPHOON**

| Date | Pilot | SN | Origin | Type | Serial | Code | Nb | Cat. |
|---|---|---|---|---|---|---|---|---|
| 29.12.44 | F/L John D. Stubbs | Aus.413275 | RAAF | Fw190 | MN265 | | 0.25 | C |
| | F/L John M. Key | RAF No.128878 | RAF | | MN267 | QC-L | 0.25 | C |
| | F/L Roger M. Stevens | RAF No.128940 | RAF | | PD613 | | 0.25 | C |
| | F/O William G. Huddart | Aus.410128 | RAAF | | JP515 | QC-X | 0.25 | C |
| 01.01.45 | F/L Howard P. Gibbons | RAF No.131023 | RAF | Fw190 | MN486 | QC-D | 1.0 | C |
| 22.01.45 | F/L Eric C.H. Vernon-Jarvis | RAF No.65545 | RAF | Bf109 | JP920 | | 1.0 | C |
| 23.01.45 | S/L Leonard H. Lambert | RAF No.119791 | RAF | Ju188 | MN265 | | 0.33 | C |
| | F/O John B.C. Catterns | RAF No.144938 | RAF | | EK140 | QC-K | 0.33 | C |
| | F/O Philip B. Noble | RAF No.161677 | RAF | | RB376 | | 0.33 | C |

**Total: 4.0**
Aircraft damaged: 7

## APPENDIX V
### AIRCRAFT LOST ON OPERATIONS

| Date | Pilot | S/N | Origin | Serial | Code | Mark | Fate |

### MUSTANG

**23.01.43**   P/O Bernard W. **KEARNEY**   Aus.405387   RAAF   **AG578**   I   †
*Took off at 13.05 for a Popular sortie with P/O Grant in the area of Beck-Stella Place (France). Failed to return. Original member of the squadron, posted from No.268 Sqn; he was completing his third sortie since June 1942. Native of Victoria, Australia.*
<u>Note on the aircraft</u>: Shipped to the UK 17.04.42. Issued to No.168 Sqn 09.11.42. Served previously with No.225 Sqn.

   P/O Ian G. **GRANT**   NZ41216   RNZAF   **AG510**   I   **PoW**
*Took off at 13.05 for a Popular sortie acting as No.2 to P/O Kearney in the area of Beck-Stella Place (France). Failed to return. Later reported as a PoW at Stalag Luft III. Original member of the squadron posted from No.268 Sqn, he was completing his third sortie since June 1942.*
<u>Note on the aircraft</u>: Shipped to the UK 30.01.42. Issued to No.168 Sqn 07.11.42. Served previously with No.241 Sqn.

**25.07.43**   P/O William A. **BRENARD**   RAF No.124379   RAF   **AM216**   I   -
*Took off at 17.00 with F/O A.J.F. Young (Mustang AM177) for a Popular sortie, Trouville - Ouistream area (France). Correct land fall was made on the French coast when, just as the photo run was started, two Fw190s were sighted. The engine of William Brenard's aircraft was hit and he baled out a few seconds later from about 1,500 feet, 10 miles from French coast. The German fighters disappeared and Arthur Young orbited over the dinghy which F/O Brenard had operated successfully. Young was ordered to return while an ASR mission was launched. Brenard was found the next day 15 miles north of Trouville and rescued by a Walrus. It was the first squadron loss since the integration into the 2<sup>nd</sup> TAF. The claim was credited to Oblt Jakob Schmidt of 3./JG 2. William Brenard returned to operations after a short leave and eventually left the squadron in February, posted to Flying Training Command.*
<u>Note on the aircraft</u>: Shipped to the UK 15.07.42. Issued to No.168 Sqn 23.06.42. Served previously with No.241 Sqn.

**07.09.43**   F/O Roderick M. **MACKENZIE**   Aus.413242   RAAF   **FD489**   IA   **Eva**.
*Took off at 14.20 acting as No.2 to F/O Leonard H. Lambert (Mustang FD545) for a tactical recce sortie over Abbeville - Amiens area (France). Landfall was made at Cayeux and photos run began. While south of Amiens for another run of photos, the section was attacked by Fw190s. On being warned by Mackenzie, the leader was engaged by 3 Fw190s in a running fight which carried him to ground level. The fight continued for some 15 minutes. When the Germans broke off, Lambert found himself near Rouen and had lost contact with Mackenzie, the last recollection he had was seeing him with a Fw190 on his tail in a steep turn. He was shot down by Lt Dietrich Kehl of 4./JG 26 but evaded capture via Spain, returning to the squadron in December, and was awarded an MBE for his escape and completed his tour the next August.*
<u>Note on the aircraft</u>: Shipped to the UK 08.10.42. Issued to No.168 Sqn 02.08.43.

**31.10.43**   2/Lt Jan G. **VON TANGEN**   N.?   RNAF   **FD554**   IA   †
*Took off at 15.00 for a low level photo of bridges over Vivier-sur-Mer (France) acting as No.2 to F/O D.A. Clifton-Mogg in Mustang FD488 with a section of No.268 Sqn. The squadron section began to take low oblique photographs over the river at Vivier-sur-Mer and set course to take another run of pictures. About 6 miles S.W. of Dol, the leader saw von Tangen turning to port to hit the ground without reasons, as no enemy opposition of any kind reported by the Desmond Clifton-Mogg. 2/Lt von Tangen, from Oslo, Norway, had joined the Squadron on 25 August 1943 posted from No.41 OTU and was completing his first sortie.*
<u>Note on the aircraft</u>: Shipped to the UK 26.11.42. Issued to No.168 Sqn 19.08.43.

**09.11.43**   P/O Graham D.L. **Machin**   RAF No.137295   RAF   **FD545**   IA   †
*Took off at 14.27 as leader to F/O Denis Clark (Mustang FD557) for a reconnaissance sortie over St-Malo (France). Failed to return, shot down by flak near Mont St-Michel. Clark had lost contact shortly before when Machin had turned sharply to port after a first run of photos around Mont St Michel. Graham Machin was in the squadron for about a year.*
Note on the aircraft: Shipped to the UK 12.11.42. Issued to No.168 Sqn 17.08.43.

**12.12.43**   F/O Kenneth S. **Ewins**   RAF No.128868   RAF   **FD534**   IA   †
*Took off at 10.56 for a reconnaissance sortie with F/O John K. Haselden (FD565). Collided in cloud with his leader and crashed near Great Dunmow, Essex, while Halsenden was able to return to base. Ewins served with the squadron since September.*
Note on the aircraft: Shipped to the UK 12.11.42. Issued to No.168 Sqn 23.07.43.

**03.01.44**   F/L Roger **Cook**   RAF No.44521   RAF   **FD445**   IA   †
*Took off at 13.00 for a Popular sortie over aerodromes around Cambrai (France). Lost in cloud by his wingman F/O Mark W.P. Smith (Mustang FD479) who continued the mission successfully. He had joined the squadron in July as supernumerary Flight Lieutenant from H.Q. No.32 Wing and had previously served with No.63 Sqn in 1942 - 1943.*
Note on the aircraft: Shipped to the UK 17.09.42. Issued to No.168 Sqn 23.06.43.

**14.01.44**   F/L Richard N.W. **Bock**   RAF No.115155   RAF   **FD542**   IA   †
*Took off at 11.00 with two others for a Popular sortie to photograph bridges in the St.Lô- Cherbourg area. Pilot encountered engine trouble and baled out 25 miles S of Ford. Pilot rescued but died later in the day from exposure. Richard Bock who had joined the squadron in May 1943 was from a British immigrant family in Chile.*
Note on the aircraft: Shipped to the UK 05.11.42. Issued to No.168 Sqn 24.09.43.

**28.02.44**   F/O Ian D. **Sheekey**   Aus.413439   RAAF   **AM105**   I   †
*Took off at 08.40 with five others for a Popular sortie around Trouville/Comsuelles-sur-Mer. Crashed on the return flight for unknown reasons 2.5 miles NW of Petersfield, Hants. The squadron had just switched back to the Mustang Mk.I two weeks previously. Native of New South Wales, Australia Ian Sheekey was first posted to No.231 Sqn in June 1943 and had just been posted in a couple of days before.*
Note on the aircraft: Shipped to the UK 14.05.42. Issued to No.168 Sqn date unrecorded. Served previously with Nos.2 and 4 Sqns.

**16.03.44**   F/O James S. **Wright**   Aus.412746   RAAF   **AM209**   I   †
*TTook off at 08.30 with F/O J.C Low RAAF (Mustang AP167) to attack a Noball target in the Gorenflos area. Lost contact with his leader, F/O John Low, RAAF and found later crashed near Ault (France). Native of New South Wales, Australia, Wright served at first with No.170 Sqn between September 1943 and January 1944 before joining the squadron.*
Note on the aircraft: Shipped to the UK 01.06.42. Issued to No.168 Sqn date unrecorded. Served previously with No.613 Sqn.

**10.04.44**   F/L Peter **Plumridge**   RAF No.89795   RAF   **AL969**   I   †
*Took off at 12.31 with three others for a Popular sortie but F/L Denis Clark who was leading the formation gave instructions to the other three to make a U-turn due to fog. Plumridge was the only one not to return, and it was found that he had crashed in the sea off Beachy Head, Sussex. He had been with the squadron since August 1943.*
Note on the aircraft: Arrived in UK 30.04.42. Issued to No.168 Sqn date unrecorded. Served previously with Nos.170 and 2 Sqns.

**06.06.44**   F/O Stanley H. **Barnard**   RAF No.114187   RAF   **AM225**   I   †
*Took off at 07.20 with three others for a Tactical reconnaissance sortie. Exploded in mid-air at 3,000 feet, 1 mile from Lion-Sur-Mer (France). Probably hit by a shell from a warship. Serving with the squadron since the previous autumn, he was from a British immigrant family in Brazil.*
Note on the aircraft: Shipped to the UK 01.06.42. Issued to No.168 Sqn 27.02.44. Served previously with No.400 (RCAF) Sqn.

**08.06.44**    F/O John C. **Low**    Aus.413129    RAAF    **AM128**    I    †

*Took off at 15.00 with three others for a Tactical reconnaissance sortie over the Beuzville/Bernay/Chateauneuf/Alençon/Sees/Argentan/Falaise/Caen area. Intercepted by Fw190s near Argentan and shot down, his victor being probably Hptm Emil Lang of III./JG 54 who claimed a Mustang shot down at low level in the area. Low was native of New South Wales, Australia and had been with the squadron since January 1943.*

Note on the aircraft: Shipped to the UK 24.05.42. Issued to No.168 Sqn date unrecorded.

**15.06.44**    F/O Roderic H. **Reeve**    RAF No.151461    **AM159**    I    -

*Took off at 05.15 for a Tactical reconnaissance sortie with three others over the Lisieux/Sees/Mortagne/L'Aigle/Bernay/Pont-L'Eveque area. Crash-landed at St-Croix for unknown reasons. Roderic Reeve had joined the squadron in October 1943. (see also operational losses - 02.08.44)*

Note on the aircraft: Shipped to the UK 14.05.42. Issued to No.168 Sqn 08.06.44. Served previously with No.2 Sqn.

**22.06.44**    F/L William K. **Dodgson**    RAF No.48177    RAF    **AG427**    I    **Eva.**

*Took off at 08.45 with three others for a Tactical reconnaissance sortie over the Cabourg/Falaise /Garnetot/Villiers-sur-Mer area. Crash-landed at St-Croix after being hit by light flak in the right fuel tank and radiator and crash-landed 10 miles N of Sees. Dodgson was a newcomer to the Squadron, being posted in on 7th June. He was a former 'Black Watch' officer transferred to the RAF in April 1942. It seems that he didn't return to the squadron.*

Note on the aircraft: Shipped to the UK 18.03.42. Issued to No.168 Sqn 08.06.44. Served previously with No.268 Sqn.

    F/O Dennis A. **Forknall**    RAF No.51065    RAF    **AP195**    I    -

*Took off at 16.00 for a Tactical reconnaissance sortie with three others over the Alençon/Mamers area. Hit by flak N.E. of Caen and force-landed at B.9, aircraft Cat.E. Forknall who was with the squadron from the beginning of the year, continuing until the end of the Battle of Normandy and when he was posted out.*

Note on the aircraft: Shipped to the UK 02.07.42. Issued to No.168 Sqn date 15.06.44.

**23.06.44**    F/L Graeme R. **Turner**    RAF No.125595    **AG513**    I    -

*Took off at 05.15 for a Tactical reconnaissance sortie with three others over the Falaise/Argentan /Sees/La Ferté Mace area. Pilot reported engine trouble and was ordered to return landing at Odiham with undercarriage unlocked. Aircraft was not repaired. Turner had joined the squadron during the month and stayed until the disbandment of the unit in February 1945.*

Note on the aircraft: Shipped to the UK 30.01.42. Issued to No.168 Sqn 23.06.43 from No.231 Sqn. Then issued to No.231 again 23.08.43. Re-issued to No.168 22.06.44.

    F/O John W. **Walker**    Aus.402988    RAAF    **AG474**    I    †

*Took off at 14.30 for a Tactical reconnaissance sortie with three others over the Falaise/Briouse/Alençon/Argentan area. Attacked by Fw190s near Falaise. Failed to return and presumed shot down by enemy fighters. Native of New South Wales, Australia, he had joined No.168 Sqn in May 1943.*

Note on the aircraft: Shipped to the UK 26.02.42. Issued to No.168 Sqn date 03.06.44. Served previously with Nos.268 and 2 Sqns.

**19.07.44**    F/O John C. **Warnock**    RAF No.127325    RAF    **AL979**    I    **Eva.**

*Took off at 19.10 for a Tactical reconnaissance sortie with F/L Charles A.M. Balbour (Mustang AP262) over the Troarn/ Doluze / St.Pierre/Livarot area. Section attacked by Bf109s of I./JG 5. Badly hit by enemy fighters and pilot baled out. Warnock, who had been posted early in the month, evaded capture but it seems that he didn't return to the squadron.*

Note on the aircraft: Shipped to the UK 07.05.42. Issued to No.168 Sqn 08.06.44 from No.2 Sqn. Served also with No.170 Sqn.

**30.07.44**    F/O John D. **Stubbs**    Aus. 413275    RAAF    **AP214**    Y    I    -

*Took off at 13.15 with F/L Leonard H. Lambert (Mustang AL973) for a low level photo recce sortie over the Beny Bocage/Viré River area. Hit by flak (37mm) over Beny bocage in the starboard tank and port ammo bin, causing ammo to explode. Pilot was able to return. Aircraft declared Cat.B but later changed for a Cat.E. Native of New South Wales, Australia, he had joined the* squadron in January 1943; later killed with squadron on 2 January 1945.

Note on the aircraft : Shipped to the UK 02.07.42. Issued to No.168 Sqn date 06.07.44. Served previously with No.169 Sqn.

**02.08.44**    F/O Roderic H. Reeve    RAF No.151461    AM169    I    -

*Took off at 15.58 for a Tactical reconnaissance sortie over the Falaise/Briouse/Alençon/Argentan area with two others. Collided with Spitfire NH272 of No.132 Sqn and crash-landed near Ryes. Pilot uninjured but aircraft destroyed by fire. Roderic Reeve left the squadron soon after that event. (See also operational losses - 15.06.44)*

Note on the aircraft : Shipped to the UK 14.05.42. Issued to No.168 Sqn 06.07.44. Served previously with Nos.169 and 63 Sqns.

**03.08.44**    F/O John B.C. Catterns    RAF No.144938    RAF    AM137    I    -

*Took off at 13.00 with F/O Philip B. Noble (Mustang AP230) for a photo reconnaissance sortie. Hit by flak and crash-landed near Caen. Catterns, who had joined the squadron during the spring, served until the end with the squadron.*

Note on the aircraft: Shipped to the UK 14.05.42. Issued to No.168 Sqn 06.07.44. Served previously with No.268 Sqn.

F/O Harold J. Panitzki    Aus.408211    RAAF    AM112    I    -

*Took off at 17.10 with F/L Arthur Young (Mustang AL973) for a photo reconnaissance sortie. Hit by flak and crash-landed at B.8. Native of Tasmania, Panitzki served with No.231 Sqn between February 1943 and January before joining the squadron. He was finally repatriated in January 1945.*

Note on the aircraft: Shipped to the UK 14.05.42. Issued to No.168 Sqn 15.06.44. Served previously with No.2 Sqn.

**07.08.44**    F/O John E. Perkins    RAF No.124852    RAF    AP193    I    -

*Took off at 12.45 for a Tactical reconnaissance sortie with F/O Philip B. Noble (Mustang AG529). Hit by flak and crash-landed at B.8. Perkins, who joined the squadron the previous spring, continued to fly with the squadron until the end of the year.*

Note on the aircraft: Shipped to the UK 02.07.42. Issued to No.168 Sqn 08.06.44. Served previously with No.16 Sqn.

**13.08.44**    S/L Druce W. Barlow    RAF No.43527    RAF    AP230    I    PoW

*Took off at 09.50 for a Tactical reconnaissance sortie over the Falaise area with F/L Mark W.P. Smith (Mustang AL995). Hit by flak and baled out. Later reported as a PoW at Stalag Luft I. S/L Barlow, who was awarded the DFC for his actions in the Middle East with No.208 Sqn, had joined No.168 Sqn the previous 23 June and was completing his 27th sortie with the squadron.*

Note on the aircraft: Shipped to the UK 16.07.42. Issued to No.168 Sqn 07.06.44. Served previously with No.613 Sqn.

**20.08.44**    F/L Denis Clark    RAF No.119758    RAF    AG346    I    †

*Took off at 16.26 with F/L Ken S. Hutchinson (Mustang AG401) for a Tactical reconnaissance sortie. Shot down by flak near Gace. He had joined the squadron in October 1943.*

Note on the aircraft: Arrived in UK 15.11.41. Issued to No.168 sqn 06.07.44, having served with No.225, 63, 26 and 16 Sqns.

**22.08.44**    F/O Patrick J. Garland    RAF No.49602    RAF    AG401    I    -

*Took off at 12.56 for a Tactical reconnaissance sortie with F/L Edgar Watson (RAAF) - Mustang AM228 -. Ran out of fuel and belly-landed 10 miles S.E. of Troan. Garland was a former 'Green Howards' officer transferred to the RAF in August 1942 and had joined the squadron two weeks before.*

Note on the aircraft: Arrived UK 10.02.42. Issued to No.168 Sqn date 10.08.44. Served previously with No.2 Sqn.

**26.09.44**    F/L Frank Bolton    RAF No.46722    RAF    AM101    K    I    †

*Took off at 17.33 for a Tactical reconnaissance sortie with F/L John E. Perkins (Mustang AM228). Attacked by mistake by P-47*

*Thunderbolts and shot down. Bolton had been with the Squadron since 10 August 1944.*
Note on the aircraft: Shipped to the UK 30.05.42. Issued to No.168 Sqn 17.08.44. Served previoulsy with No.169 Sqn.

## TYPHOON

**26.11.44**   F/L John K. **BROWN**   RAF No.133019   **JP677**   QC-P   IB   **Inj.**
*Took off at 15.10 with four others for an escort of VIPs to England. Crash-landed on the beach, Brighton, Sussex. Pilot injured and taken to Haywards Heath Hospital with fractured skull, concussion and lacerated forehead. Brown had joined the squadron early in the month.*
Note on the aircraft: TOC No.51 MU 24.08.43. Issued to No.168 Sqn 26.10.44. Served previously with Nos.1 and 137 Sqns.

**24.12.44**   F/O Derek G. **DICKSON**   RAF No.151456   RAF   **JP919**   IB   **PoW**
*Took off at 13.25 with eight others for an armed recce over the Malmedy area. Hit by flak near Malmedy (Belgium) and was last seen smoking and climbing into sun. Later reported as a PoW, he had joined the squadron at the end of 1943.*
Note on the aircraft: TOC No.20 MU 27.09.43. Issued to No.168 Sqn 12.10.44. Served previously with No.193 Sqn.

**26.12.44**   F/O Vasco O. **GILBERT**   RAF No.136832   RAF   **EJ946**   IB   †
*Took off at 15.20 for an armed recce over the Prum area with seven others led by F/L Stubbs. Failed to return after attacking 5 METs under heavy flak. Gilbert was a newcomer to the squadron, posted in two days earlier.*
Note on the aircraft: TOC No.18 MU 12.03.43. Issued to No.168 Sqn 26.10.44. Served previously with Nos.175, 183 & 266 Sqns.

**29.12.44**   F/L Ernest **GIBBONS**   RAF No.124498   RAF   **JR332**   IB   †
*Took off at 10.05 for an armed reconnaissance with eight others, F/L Stubbs leading. At 10.50 the formation was jumped by 12 Fw190s 'Long nose' of III./JG 54 led by the German ace Hptm 'Bazi' Weiss and he was shot down S.W. of Steinfurt. Last seen spinning in at 1,500 ft after being attacked. He had been with the squadron since October.*
Note on the aircraft: TOC No.20 MU 15.11.43. Issued to No.168 Sqn 12.10.44. Served previously with No.609 Sqn.

F/L Roy F. **PLANT**   RAF No.135149   **MN639**   QC-S   IB   **PoW**
*See above. Later reported as a PoW. During that combat No.168 Sqn pilots were able in return to claim one confirmed victory against a Fw190 and two others damaged (Huddart and Key). Plant had joined the squadron the previous month.*
Note on the aircraft: TOC No.51 MU 25.04.44. Issued to No.168 Sqn 12.10.44. Served previously with No.181 Sqn.

**01.01.45**   F/L Howard P. **GIBBONS**   RAF No.131023   RAF   **MN486**   QC-D   IB   †
*F/L Gibbons was on air test over the airfield when aircraft of JG 3 appeared and strafe the airfield during Operation 'Bodenplatte'. He was seen to shoot down a Fw190, but his Typhoon was then attacked by three Bf109s and he was shot down and killed. He had been with the squadron since July.*
Note on the aircraft: TOC No.51 MU 18.03.44. Issued to No.168 Sqn 28.10.44. Served previously with No.184 Sqn.

**22.01.45**   F/O William G. **HUDDART**   Aus.410128   RAAF   **RB361**   IB   †
*Took off at 15.30 for an armed recce over the Donsten/Dulmen area with five others and the formation attacked four trains. Huddart was last seen diving down to attack a train, deliver his attack and to pull out. Huddart was an Australian, from Victoria, and had served with No.170 Sqn between August 1943 and January 1944 before joining No.168 Sqn.*
Note on the aircraft: TOC No.51 MU 23.11.44. Issued to No.168 Sqn 11.01.45.

**02.02.45**   F/O Thomas **Lowe**   RAF No.148903   RAF   **MN265**   IB   **Eva.**
*Took off at 09.50 with 7 others for an armed recce over the Dulmen/Mubster/Paderborne area. The formation was led by the CO, S/L Lambert. Lowe experienced engine failure over Panderborne and force-landed. He reported by radio that he was OK and waiting for the Russians. In this operation, two locos and two wagons were damaged. Lowe had arrived at the squadron the previous month.*
<u>Note on the aircraft</u>: TOC No.20 MU 26.02.44. Issued to No.168 Sqn 18.01.45. Served previously with Nos.3 & 268 Sqns.

**03.02.45**   S/L Eric C.H. **Vernon-Jarvis**   RAF No.65545   RAF   **RB270**   IB   †
*Took off at 10.55 for an armed recce in the Rheine/Osnabruck/Herford/Bielfeld/Hamm area, leading seven more Typhoons. Hit by flak while attacking a train the tail of his Typhoon was bloewn by flak, with the tail blowing off. S/L Vernon-Jarvis had just taken command of the Squadron from S/L Lambert. S/L Vernon-Jarvis had been awarded the DFC the previous October for his actions with No.175 Sqn and had been posted in on 16.01.45 to replace S/L Lambert. He also served with No.193 Sqn. Consequently Lambert had to remain in command until a new CO could be appointed but the Squadron was disbanded before this occurred.*
<u>Note on the aircraft</u>: TOC No.51 MU 27.09.43. Issued to No.168 Sqn 25.01.45.

*Total: 38*

## APPENDIX VI
### Aircraft Lost in Accidents

### Tomahawk

**06.08.42**   P/O Robert K.A. **Andrew**   NZ412010   RNZAF   **AH891**   IIA   †
*Lost its port wing on striking tree while carrying out a low level dummy attack on gun emplacements at 12.30 along the Thetford-Watton road, near Thetford, Norfolk. The aircraft flicked over once or twice before fitting the gorund some 200 yards on and caught fire. Andrew was serving No.268 Sqn before being posted to No.168 Sqn on formation.*
<u>Note on the aircraft</u>: TOC NO.8 MU 14.12.40. Issued to No.168 Sqn 12.07.42 from No.400 (RCAF) Sqn. Served also previously with Nos.403 (RCAF) Sqn.

### Typhoon

**02.01.45**   F/L John D. **Stubbs**   Aus. 413275   RAAF   **RB209**   IB   †
*Swung on take-off for air test and hit Typhoon MP201, Eindhovern, Holland. (See also entry 30.07.44).*
<u>Note on the aircraft</u> : TOC No.5 MU 30.09.44. Issued to No.168 Sqn date unrecordeed

*Total: 2*

## APPENDIX VII
### Aircraft serial numbers matching with individual letters

**EK-A/OE-A/A/QC-A**
AP176 (*Mustang I*)

**EK-B/OE-B/B/QC-B**

**EK-C/OE-C/C/QC-C**

**EK-D/OE-D/D/QC-D**
MN486 (*Typhoon*)

**EK-E/OE-E/E/QC-E**

**EK-F/OE-F/F/QC-F**

**EK-G/OE-G/G/QC-G**

**EK-H/OE-H/H/QC-H**

**EK-I/OE-I/I/QC-I**

**EK-J/OE-J/J/QC-J**

**EK-K/OE-K/K/QC-K**
AM101 (*Mustang I*)
EK140 (*Typhoon*)

**EK-L/OE-L/L/QC-L**
MN267 (*Typhoon*)

**EK-M/OE-M/M/QC-M**
AG529 (*Mustang I*)
MN607 (*Typhoon*)

**EK-N/ON-N/N/QC-N**
AH775 (*Tomahawk*)

**EK-O/OE-O/O/QC-O**

**EK-P/OE-P/P/QC-P**
JP677 (*Typhoon*)

**EK-Q/OE-Q/Q/QC-Q**
EJ946 (*Typhoon*)

**EK-R/OE-R/R/QC-R**
AL973 (*Mustang I*)

**EK-S/OE-S/S/QC-S**
MN639 (*Typhoon*)

**EK-T/OE-T/T/QC-T**

**EK-U/OE-U/U/QC-U**

**EK-V/OE-V/V/QC-V**

**EK-W/OE-W/W/QC-W**
MM976 (*Typhoon*)

**EK-X/OE-X/X/QC-X**
JP515 (*Typhoon*)

**EK-Y/OE-Y/Y/QC-Y**

**EK-Z/OE-Z/Z/QC-Z**

Note: No squadron code for the Mustangs.

## APPENDIX VIII
### LIST OF KNOWN PILOTS POSTED OR ATTACHED TO THE SQUADRON

### RAAF
D.A. **Bleechmore**, Aus.416407
W.G. **Huddart**, Aus.410128
B.W. **Kearney**, Aus.405387
J.C. **Low**, Aus.413129
R.M. **Mackenzie**, Aus.413242
H.J. **Panitzki**, Aus.408211
R.R. **Sanderson**, Aus.400836
I.D. **Sheekey**, Aus.413439
J.D. **Stubbs**, Aus.413275
J.W. **Walker**, Aus.402988
A.E. **Watson**, Aus.408543
J.S. **Wright**, Aus.412746

### RAF
D.W. **Barlow**, RAF No.43527
C.H. **Barbour**, RAF No.120863
J.H. **Bangs**, RAF No.177294
F.N. **Bantfort**, RAF No.44534
S.H. **Barnard**, RAF No.144187, BRAZIL
R.A. **Bethell**, RAF No.120413
A.G. **Bird**, RAF No.119122
R.N.W. **Bock**, RAF No.115155, CHILE
F. **Bolton**, RAF No.46722
D.A. **Bourne**, RAF No.115107
R.I.M. **Bowen**, RAF No.25118
W.A. **Brenard**, RAF No.124379
W.M. **Brooke-Taylor**, RAF No.44159
J.K. **Brown**, RAF No.133019
R.C.J. **Cainan**, RAF No.1319612
M.W. **Canham**, RAF No.131026
G.W. **Carr**, RAF No.158916
J.B.C. **Catterns**, RAF No.144938
D. **Clark**, RAF No.119758
D.A. **Clifton-Mogg**, RAF No.122932
R. **Cook**, RAF No.44521
J.R. **Colville**, RAF No.137172
D. **Cormack**, RAF No.48789
S. **Cromarty-Dickson**, RAF No.88744
D.G. **Dickson**, RAF No.151456
N.L. **Dimond**, RAF No.137419
W.K. **Dodgson**, RAF No.48777
P. **Edelsten**, RAF No.128855
A. **Edmonds**, RAF No.111231
H.T. **Elliott**, RAF No.126967
K.S. **Ewins**, RAF No.128868
D.N. **Fearon**, RAF No.41389
A.B. **Field**, RAF No.128928
D.A. **Forknall**, RAF No.51065
B.N.E. **Ford-Coates**, RAF No.128880
P.J. **Garland**, RAF No.49602
R.G. **Gent**, RAF No.115226
E. **Gibbons**, RAF No.124498
H.P. **Gibbons**, RAF No.131023
V.O. **Gilbert**, RAF No.136832
M.J. **Gray**, RAF No.106182
D.A. **Greville-Heygate**, RAF No.112011
A.L.S. **Hallett**, RAF No.126642
N.T. **Harris**, RAF No.118568
J.K. **Haselden**, RAF No.79795
C.G. **Hubah**, RAF No.133642, WEST INDIES
K.S. **Huskinson**, RAF No.48526
G.J. **Hussey**, RAF No.150010, NEW ZEALAND
S.J. **Huxley**, RAF No.144008
B.J. **Jennings**, RAF No.47706
J.M. **Key**, RAF No.128878
M.D. **Khan**, RAF No.119569, IRELAND
L.H. **Lambert**, RAF No.119791
D.E. **Love**, RAF No.128128
T. **Lowe**, RAF No.148903
G.D.L. **Machin**, RAF No.137295
P.W. **Mason**, RAF No.41721
E.J. **Milne**, RAF No.122226
T.E.D. **Mitchell**, RAF No.49740
P.D. **Morris**, RAF No.43551
C. de B. **Newcomb**, RAF No.1382089
P.B. **Noble**, RAF No.161677
D.A.D.L. **Nichols**, RAF No.72002
A.M. **Peake**, RAF No.122230
H.J. **Perkins**, RAF No.124852
R.F. **Plant**, RAF No.135149
P. **Plumridge**, RAF No.89795
R.H. **Reeve**, RAF No.151461
M.A. **Richardson**, RAF No.115442
M.G. **Ridley-Martin**, RAF No.47442
J.G. **Seth-Smith**, RAF No.47545
J.B. **Skinner**, RAF No.171585
M.W.P. **Smith**, RAF No.116748
E. **Spencer**, RAF No.132758
R.M. **Stevens**, RAF No.128940
B. **Thirtle**, RAF No.67065
R.F. **Turner**, RAF No.125595
J.W. **Vane**, RAF No.146429
E.H.A. **Vernon-Jarvis**, RAF No.65545
J.C. **Warnock**, RAF No.127325
G.F. **Watson-Smyth**, RAF No.25069
P. **Weeden**, RAF No.128866
P. **Wicks**, RAF No.106514
A.J.F. **Young**, RAF No.116448

### RNAF
J.G. **von Tangen**, N.?

### RNZAF
R.K.A. **Andrew**, NZ412010
J.H. **Davies**, NZ439003
I.G. **Grant**, NZ41216
S.J. **Shayle-George**, NZ412745
W.S. **Watson**, NZ412769

## APPENDIX IX
## ROLL OF HONOUR
✝

### AIRCREW

| Name | Service No | Rank | Age | Origin | Date | Serial |
|---|---|---|---|---|---|---|
| **ANDREW**, Robert Kent Anderson | NZ412010 | P/O | 24 | RNZAF | 06.08.42 | AH891 |
| **BARNARD**, Stanley Harry[1] | RAF No.114187 | F/O | 22 | RAF | 06.06.44 | AM225 |
| **BOCK**, Richard Norman Walker[2] | RAF No.115155 | F/L | 23 | RAF | 14.01.44 | FD542 |
| **BOLTON**, Frank | RAF No.46722 | F/L | 29 | RAF | 26.09.44 | AM101 |
| **CLARK**, Denis | RAF No.119758 | F/L | 25 | RAF | 25.08.44 | AG346 |
| **COOK**, Roger | RAF No.44521 | F/L | 24 | RAF | 03.01.44 | FD445 |
| **EWINS**, Kenneth Sidney | RAF No.128868 | F/O | 22 | RAF | 12.12.43 | FD534 |
| **GIBBONS**, Ernest | RAF No.124498 | F/L | 30 | RAF | 29.12.44 | JR332 |
| **GIBBONS**, Howard Plaistone | RAF No.131023 | F/L | 24 | RAF | 01.01.45 | MN486 |
| **GILBERT**, Vasco Ortigzo | RAF No.136832 | F/O | 27 | RAF | 26.12.44 | EJ946 |
| **HUDDART**, William Grayson | Aus.410128 | F/O | 22 | RAAF | 22.01.45 | RB361 |
| **KEARNEY**, Bernard Wilson | Aus.405387 | P/O | 25 | RAAF | 23.01.43 | AG578 |
| **LOW**, John Charles | Aus.413129 | F/O | 28 | RAAF | 08.06.44 | AM128 |
| **MACHIN**, Graham Dudley Launcelot | RAF No.137295 | P/O | 22 | RAF | 09.11.43 | FD545 |
| **PLUMRIDGE**, Peter | RAF No.89795 | F/L | 22 | RAF | 10.04.44 | AL969 |
| **SHEEKEY**, Ian Douglas | Aus.413439 | F/O | 24 | RAAF | 28.02.44 | AM105 |
| **STUBBS**, John Douglas | Aus.413275 | F/L | 29 | RAAF | 02.01.45 | RB209 |
| **von TANGEN**, Jan Gert | N.? | 2/Lt | n/k | RNAF | 31.10.43 | FD554 |
| **VERNON-JARVIS**, Eric Horace Anthony | RAF No.65545 | S/L | n/k | RAF | 03.02.45 | RB270 |
| **WALKER**, John William | Aus.402988 | F/O | 30 | RAAF | 23.06.44 | AG474 |
| **WRIGHT**, James Stuart | Aus.412746 | F/O | 26 | RAAF | 16.03.44 | AM209 |

[1] From Brazil.
[2] From Chile.

**Total: 21**

Australia: 7
New Zealand: 1
Norway: 1
United Kingdom: 12

### GROUNDCREW

| Name | Service No | Rank | Age | Origin | Date | Serial |
|---|---|---|---|---|---|---|
| **DAVIES**, Evan | RAF No.1510193 | LAC | 23 | RAF | 01.01.45 | - |
| **EARLDLEY**, Albert Rudolph Osborne* | Can./R.113988 | Corp | 36 | RCAF | 02.01.45 | - |
| **GOSNEY**, John Raymond | RAF No.573061 | Sgt | 22 | RAF | 01.01.45 | - |
| **JONES**, Frank Thomas | RAF No.1593298 | Sgt | n/k | RAF | 21.06.44 | - |
| **NICHOLSON**, Geoffrey William | RAF No.1722813 | LAC | n/k | RAF | 01.01.45 | - |

*Died of wounds sustained the previous day.

**Total: 5**

Canada: 1
United Kingdom: 4

n/k: not known

As with many army co-operation units, the Tomahawk was selected to replace the vulnerable Lysander. The aircraft gave the opportunity to the new pilots to train on single-engine fighters pending delivery of the Mustang. Although, by 1942, the Tomahawk was widespread used with Army Co-operation Command, few operational missions were actually undertaken by the squadrons so-equipped. Here is a Tomahawk Mk.I, AH775, flying over the British countryside during summer 1942. It is wearing the new squadron letter code 'OE' which had replaced the earlier 'EK' codes which were used for a couple of weeks only in mid-1942.

Fewer than 100 Mustang Mk.IAs were taken on charge by the RAF, the rest of the order being seized by the Americans when they entered into war and only a very few units including No.168 Sqn were fully equipped with the type and only for a short time. The main difference compared to the Mk.I was the armament, four 20-mm cannons instead of the machine-guns. If the cannons were a powerful set, they didn't offer a real advantage to the Mk.I as the primary mission was to bring back valuable photographs and avoid as far as possible any skirmish with the Luftwaffe.

Above and below: Mustang Mk.Is of No.168 Sqn were filmed while operating from B.21 (Ste-Honorine-de-Ducy) on 23 August 1944. It was a busy day for the squadron with 26 sorties recorded between 12.05 and 19.53. Above, F/L Bolton is ready to go with AM101/K, while below F/L Lambert is taking off on board AL973/R under the hot summer sun of Normandy. Take-off time is recorded as being 13.59. F/L Lambert led the two aircraft over a sector where no major observations were made and both Mustangs landed back at base at 15.10.

Above, AG529 has just landed while on the left, another Mustang, coded 'N' is taking off with a typical landscape of Normandy behind.

Below: Two Typhoons landing at B.78 Eindhoven (Netherlands) in December 1944, MN639/QC-S and Ek140/QC-K. Being used as fighters, No.168 Squadron Typhoons did not carry any racks under the wings.
(*Chris Thomas and Andrew Thomas*)

Above: Two mechanics handling the camera installed on the tactical reconnaissance Mustang located behind the cockpit in a port oblique position. It was a Type F.24 (8") camera.

Left: The hero of the day, F/L Howard Gibbons, who had just got airborne from Eindhoven on an air test on the infamous day of 1 January 1945 when the fighters of JG 3 swept in. He managed to shoot the tail off an Fw190 but he didn't have time to celebrate his success as he fell to the guns of two Bf109s a couple of minutes later. (*Chris Thomas*)

Below: Pilots of No.168 Squadron relaxing under an apple tree at B.8/Sommervieu in Normandy during a break from operations in early July 1944, with the Mustangs behind waiting at dispersal for the next sortie.

## Summary of the operational activity
## No.168 Squadron

| A/C types | First sortie | Last sortie | Total sorties | Tot type | A/c Lost Op | A/c Lost Acc | Tot. | Tot. type | Claims | V-1 | Pilot † | PoWs | Eva. |
|---|---|---|---|---|---|---|---|---|---|---|---|---|---|
| Tomahawk I | - | - | - | - | - | - | - | - | - | - | - | - | - |
| Tomahawk IIA | - | - | - | - | - | 1 | 1 | 1 | - | - | 1 | - | - |
| Mustang I | 07.12.42 | (16.08.43) | 206 | 1,957 | 3 | - | 3 | 23 | - | - | 1 | 1 | - |
| | (14.02.44) | 30.09.44 | 1,751 | | 20 | - | 20 | | - | - | 8 | 1 | 2 |
| Mustang IA | 11.08.43 | 12.02.44 | 245 | 245 | 6 | - | 6 | 6 | - | - | 5 | - | 1 |
| Typhoon IB | 12.10.44 | 28.02.45 | 985 | 985 | 9 | 1 | 10 | 10 | 4.0 | - | 6 | 2 | 1 |
| Others | - | - | - | - | - | - | - | - | - | - | - | - | - |
| Compilation | 07.12.42 | 28.02.45 | 3,187 | | 38 | 2 | 40 | 40 | 4.0 | - | 21 | 4 | 4 |

**Main Awards**

**DSO:** -

**DFC: 11**

**DFM:** -

*Points of interest :*
- Last squadron equiped with Typhoons.
- First Typhoon squadron disbanded.
- No RCAF flying personnel served with the squadron.

*Unsolved mystery*
None.

*Statistics :*
- Lost one aircraft every 84 sorties (Mustang - 76; Typhoon - 109.5).
- 5.00 % of the combat aircraft losses occured during non operational flights, well below the average.

## BADGE
In front of a scroll, a flaming arrow, pointing downwards.

*The arrow symbolises attack and the scroll information transmitted as a result of reconnaissance.*

## MOTTO
*RERUM COGNOSCERE CAUSAS*

*TO KNOW THE CAUSE OF THINGS*

**Authority: King George VI, January 1945**

**Curtiss Tomahawk Mk. I AH775, Bottisham, Summer 1942.**
Taken on charge in UK on 17 April 1941, AH 775 first served with No.268 Sqn and was among the few aircraft transferred to No.168 Sqn when it was formed from a nucleus of No.268 Sqn personel and material. AH775 was officially issued to No.168 Sqn on 9 July 1942. The Tomahawk remained with the squadron until 29 December 1942 when it was sent to No.8 MU as the squadron was undertaking its conversion on Mustangs. No.168 Sqn did not carry out a single sortie on Tomahawk.

**North American Mustang Mk.I AP176, Odiham, Summer 1943.**
Arriving in UK on 7 Februar 1942, AP176 was stored at No.12 MU after its conversion to tactical reconnaissance aircraft and was issued to No.168 Sqn on 20 February 1943 and performed its first operational sortie on 26th May with F/L Peter D. Morris in command. Twenty-six more sorties followed before the squadron switch to Mustang Mk.IA. On 26 August 1943, AP176 was sent to No.400 (RCAF) Sqn keeping its individual letter 'A' before returning to the squadon in Spring 1944. It resumed operations on 30 April 1944. AP176 flew intensively in May and June 1944 flying 14 sorties, the last recorded being on 15th June when S/L Percy W. Mason took off for a tactical recce over Domfront-Viré-Mortagne. It is not sure what happened next to AP176 but it was sent for repairs in UK on 26 June and once completed stored at No.38 MU from 5 October onwards. It was officially struck off charge on 19 March 1947, but its true fate after its arrival at No.38 MU is not known.

**North American Mustang Mk.I AP214, B.8 Sommervieu, France, June 1944.**

Arriving in UK on 2 July 1942, AP214 was first stored at No.20 MU before to be issued to No.169 Sqn on 31 December 1942 being used until end of next summer. But just before No.169 Sqn was disbanded, AP214 was sent for repairs and then stored. It was allocated again in June 1944 when it was taken on charge by No.168 Sqn that month via No.83 GSU which took officially on charge AP214 on 10 June 1944. No precise date is given for the arrival at No.168 Sqn, but AP214 made a first operational sortie on 21st June flown by F/O Derek G. Dickson. During the following weeks, it flew 33 others tactical reconnaissance sorties including 4 sorties on 18th July. However on 30 July 1944, it was damaged by flak while flown by F/O John D. Stubbs (RAAF) - see operational losses. First declared Cat. B, that was finally changed for Cat. E on the following 28 August.

**North American Mustang Mk.I AG529, B.21 Ste-Honorine, France, August 1944.**

First reported on Bristish soil on 14 March 1942, AG529 was issued to No.268 Sqn on 3 June 1942. By Spring 1944, it has been allocated to No.39 Wing and on 6 July 1944 was taken on charge by No.168 Sqn but it is believed that it was damaged in a non operational flight soon after, before it could carry out any operational flight. Sent for repairs at No.400 R&SU it returned to the squadron on 27 July, and F/O Roderic H. Reeve was the pilot who took it for a its first sortie with the squadron the same day. The next day it completed 4 sorties, and then 3 more on the 29 July and until the 26 September 1944 when F/L William K. Dodgson, a former officer Black Watch, took off for a last tactical reconnaissance sortie. AG529 achieved in all 36 sorties with No.168 Sqn. AG529 was eventually struck off charge on 9 October 1944 soon after its departure from the squadron. The small triangle above the fin flash is the No.151 RU badge, indicating a repair by that unit.

**Hawker Typhoon Mk.IB MN639, Flight Lieutenant Roy Plant, B.78 Eindhoven (Netherlands), 29 December 1944.**

Reported on charge at No.51 MU on 24 April 1944 it was first allocated to No.181 Sqn as 'EL-E'. Damaged in action on 30 June, the repairs were completed by 19 August followed by storage. It was issued to No.168 Sqn in October and became 'QC-S', by 12th of that month and was flown by various pilots. It was damaged by an accident on 12 November but was back with the Squadron on 30 November. On 29 December 1944 MN639 was shot down by enemy fighters after attacking a locomotive near Steinfurt and F/L Roy F. Plant was taken PoW. MN639 was fitted with a 4-bladed propeller and a large tailplane. It is known that some No.168 Sqn Typhoons had their spinners painted in yellow, but its general use is unconfirmed.

**Hawker Typhoon Mk.IB JP515, B.78 Eindhoven (Netherlands), February 1945.**

JP515 was first reported on 17 July 1943, with No.181 Sqn. Coded 'EL-T', it flew with that unit until it went for canopy modifications, probably at Cunliffe Owen or Hawker, on 12 June 1944. These were complete by 24 August and JP515 was eventually issued to No.168 Sqn by 30 November 1944, becoming 'QC-X' and was flown by various pilots. On 3 February 1945, on returning from an armed recce, JP515 left the runway and hit soft ground, flipping over on to its back. The pilot, F/L Norman T. Harris, although injured, was fortunate to survive as several Typhoon pilots lost their lives in this type of accident. The aircraft was declared Cat. B and returned to the UK for repair by Taylorcraft. This was completed by 13 April and JP515 was reported at No.5 MU, Kemble, a week later; stored until September 1946 it was then allocated to No.2 SoTT as 6134M. However this allocation was cancelled and JP515 was soc as scrap the following month.

www.ingramcontent.com/pod-product-compliance
Lightning Source LLC
Chambersburg PA
CBHW041542040426